Finding Anna

A True Story of Child Sexual Abuse

(The Revised Edition)

Trish Kaye Lleone

Copyright Trish Kaye Lleone 2014

Published by Trish Kaye Lleone at Smashwords

© 2014 Trish Kaye Lleone

All Rights Reserved. No part of this publication may be reproduced, distributed, or transmitted in any form or by any means, including photocopying, recording, or other electronic or mechanical methods, without the prior written permission of the publisher, except in the case of brief quotations embodied in critical reviews and certain other noncommercial uses permitted by copyright law. For permission requests, write to the publisher, addressed "Attention: Permissions Coordinator," at the addresses below.

Trish Kaye Lleone

www.findinganna.com

ACKNOWLEDGMENTS

This book would not have been possible without the people who cheered me on, put up with my mood swings and who believed in me. I would like to acknowledge the following people:

Jonathan Sturak, you rock! Thank you so much for agreeing to go through my first draft, for editing it and for your very inspiring review. Your support and encouragement fueled my desire to see this book to publication and I am forever grateful.

Matt Himmel, my Twitter friend, indeed I hope someday we would meet in person and get to give each other a hug. From the bottom of my heart, I thank you for your friendship and for agreeing to read the final draft of this novelette. Your kind words are uplifting.

My utmost gratitude to Ruben, Lalaine, Sophie and little David for always being there for me. Ben and Laine, your affections for this lost soul will eternally be cherished.

To my best friend Jenie de Leon, this world is a much better place because of you. Thank you for the gift of friendship. You are beautiful inside and out.

***

Dedication

For Jane Marilyn.

I pray that life had been kind to you all these years...

For Sarah,

I am forever thankful for your warmth and love.

For Isidoro,

Though fate did not allow for our paths to cross, I hold you dear to my heart.

***

Prologue

I'm a survivor. And I say this with so much pride I could burst into a million tiny pieces at your feet. I've been fighting battles since I was born. My first major victory was when I stayed alive long enough to reach the hospital the day I made my world debut. And then, both gigantic and little victories sprinkled the rest of my growing up years molding me into becoming the headstrong woman I am today. Not all of my battles resulted in triumphs, of course I also have losses and do have scars to show for each defeat but these losses keep me going. My downfalls fuel my fire to fight through life's challenges and to have compassion for the weak. I have a tenacious spirit, I may fall, get broken, battered and bruised, but I never give up.

I am a woman full of passion. I am passionate about the things that I believe in like equality, free will, justice and love. It is these passions that drive me to keep breathing when life throws me down.

When I want something so bad I could taste it in my mouth, I work hard to get it. I can push myself to the wall, cross boundaries and defy social conventions when I am on a quest to achieving my goal. I am never afraid of taking risks because I believe that taking risks is the only way for me to find out what's on the other side.

I abhor being caged, hence I hate being confined within conventions and having to stick to rules. These things snatch away little joys in life, in my opinion. The playful, mischievous side of me thinks that walking straight lines is boring and too restricting.

I am impulsive and adventurous. My take on the world is that it was created to be explored and enjoyed. I would love to see the magnificent beauty of the Alps, experience the sun in Tuscany, embrace the quiet life in Sicily, cruise along the narrow roads of Monaco and discover my ancient roots in Israel. Sometimes I wish was athletic enough to bungee jump or engage in extreme sports. But I do have such a faint heart for anything that involves heights and defying gravity so I'd rather just run, swim or bike.

Anyway, I digress....

My intentions are often misconstrued, while I am genuine in my relations with people, my fear of rejection makes me instinctively put up a wall of reservation around me, particularly in expressing my thoughts and emotions. I do have solid trust issues, which is a result of being abandoned twice in my life - first by my mother and second by my (fortunately) ex-husband.

I have a deep craving to be loved, needed and nurtured. I think everyone else has that longing. This is probably the reason why I love like there is no tomorrow and there is always that need in me to please the people I care so much about.

Beneath my 5 feet 2 inch frame lies a soul that wants nothing more than the simple joys of life. In a world replete with commercialism, materialism and skewed ideologies, I am one of the very few who stand in the midst of it all wanting nothing more than to watch sunsets and sunrises with the man I love, to wake up every single day with the knowledge that there are people who see me for who I really am - a woman both of strength and weaknesses - and still love me anyway. I'd like to live each day and not just survive it and I hope to someday find my own peaceful corner - a little nook void of confusion, insecurities and heartbreaks.

This is me, summed up into hundreds of words that I could muster to use to describe the person behind my name. If I would be asked to write about who I am in two sentences, this is probably what I would come up with:

"I am a fireball of emotions and impulses; my zest for life is unquenchable. And I am either of only two things: Fire or Ice."

-Trish Kaye Lleone

***

Chapter 1

I made my world debut in 1976. I was told that my mother gave birth to me, aided by a local midwife, in a two story wooden house which sat in the heart of a pulsating, vibrant and culturally diverse city. She called this house a "home" for a few years, paying rental fee month after month while she sometimes stayed at home to care for me and on nights when it was scarce, she worked as a bar girl. Yes, my mother was a prostitute. She traded her body and sexual expertise for money to survive.

Later on, I would find out that she didn't have to do what she did if only she returned to her hometown. My mother is the daughter of a Jewish Chemical Engineer who tried to establish a loving father-daughter relationship with her when she was young, but my mother was a renegade. She hated being confined at home, she didn't like having to follow rules, she intentionally missed her classes in school and went out with her friends during school days, while the rest of her classmates would be in their classrooms laboring on their grades, my mother would be in the movie houses or in the company of like-minded young boys and girls drinking beer, singing and smoking. This created a dent in her relationship with my grandfather, so she ran away from home. No one else knows what happened between the time she left home and the time she started engaging in the sex trade industry, except her. My grandfather died in 1986 and he never had a chance to see his eldest daughter again. Whether it was out of banal pride, shame or hate, only she knows. But what I am sure of is that my mother made choices in life that left in its path a string of shattered dreams and broken hearts.

The house my mother had chosen to live in was old and almost dilapidated, but it probably was cheap enough for her to be able to afford. But more than that, it was extremely close to my father's house. Eventually however, we moved out and relocated into a tiny, dingy apartment in the outskirts of the city because it was cheaper and because my mother's relationship with my father started going downhill. Much of my memories with my mother happened in this apartment we moved into; hence, we probably lived in it for many years.

When I was eighteen, my father showed me the first house. "That's where you were born," he said. I stood from across the road gazing at the old, wooden structure with its huge capiz-lined windows and rusty tin roof, and imagined what it must have looked like inside on the night I was born. Briefly, I imagined my mother's pregnant body lying helplessly on the floor as she writhed and wriggled in labor pains while a local midwife sat in between my mother's spread legs as she coaxed her patient to push, breathe and push. A single, yellow bulb bathed the room with light from above their heads and for what seemed like hours, a shrill voice tore through the still dead of the night indicating that I had been born and the woman's laborious screams of pain finally stopped.

"Let's go?" my father asked, a clear call back to earth. I wanted to ask how I was born, was it just as how I imagined it? But I kept silent as I hopped back into the car. Why my father brought me to that place remains a mystery to me. All I knew was that when I turned eighteen, he took me on an adventure to search for the missing link in my life and we failed. Perhaps it was his attempt at closure, or perhaps it was his attempt at killing my mother's character in me.

The circumstances surrounding my birth are like pieces of a puzzle to me even to this day. I was told that on the night I was born, I had to be rushed to the hospital because I had congenital pulmonary issues and my fingernails and toenails were blue, hence I grew up knowing that I was born a blue baby. Apparently, another woman helped my mother that night and that woman became my mother just a few months before I turned seven. No, I wasn't adopted. I was given up.

My mother - let's call her Anna - met my father when he was already married. Well, Anna fell in love despite the knowledge that Papa already had a family and could never make an honest woman out of her. Thinking about it now, it's probably in the genes, this stubbornness and this devil-may-care attitude. I see myself in Anna often and it scares the living daylights out of me because, truth be told, I do not want to be like her. But in so many ways, I am like her and no matter how I try my best to stay out of her memories' shadows, it seems that I am imprisoned there. My pre-adolescent and teenage years were a series of highs and lows as I struggled to prove to the world that despite the blood that runs through me, I am not my mother. Every day was a war waged towards veering away from her shadows.

Anyway, Anna and Papa's love affair seemed to have flourished because it produced me. I am a "love-child", their love-child. Whether I was a welcomed bundle of surprise or not was a mystery that I sought out to solve. There were a lot of times when I felt that Papa hated me. I could not remember a time that he ever carried me on his lap or sang me lullabies. I could not even remember him talking to me except on those times he would scold me for misbehaving. It was difficult to grow up knowing you have a father that you cannot run to when your knees got scraped or to ask for counsel when you're facing crossroads. It was even more difficult to grow up feeling lost and uncertain every day.

Much like the circumstances surrounding my birth, my childhood memories were also like jigsaw puzzles that I struggle to piece together. When I try to remember, all I could come up with are bits and pieces of memories that I could not string together in chronological order. I see faces - women, men, and children. I see places - a nipa hut, a large square space that had no rooms. I see my father shaving my mother's head, I see my mother crying, begging my father to let me out of this big family home so she can take me home with her. I see a man who owned a television store. I see a man who bought me new clothes for Christmas and spent one Christmas eve with me and Anna in our apartment. I see Anna, drunk and in a fit of drunken rage being dragged by four men into a room with mirrors and dresses lying everywhere. I see Anna and her friends sitting in our "living room" smoking pot. And then I see Anna banging her protruding belly on the wall. None of my early childhood memories were consistent; there were always different names, different places, different faces and different surroundings. Thinking about it now, I was probably shuttled in between one caretaker to another more than I ever spent time with Anna.

But I loved her. I loved her with all the love that my tiny being could muster. She was the most beautiful woman I had ever laid eyes on. Anna had honey brown curls, no matter how long she grew her hair or how short she would cut it, she was beautiful. I remember her sporting a mullet hairstyle one time and I was mesmerized by the golden streaks that the sunlight's reflection created on her crown. Her mere presence beside me drowned out the city's enticing sights, smells and sounds. Its rows of colorful shops, sparkling street lights, booming traffic and various gastronomical offerings which I rarely come to witness failed to interest me. I was held captive by the sun's reflection dancing and playing with the shades of brown on her head. "You look like an angel, Mama," I whispered, wide-eyed, as the horse-drawn carriage we were riding on blazed across the city's avenues.

"And you look like a cherub." She smiled down at me and reached over to smoothen my baby doll dress. I looked down on my pale yellow skirt, a hand-me-down from one of Anna's friend's daughters, its lacy hem covered my knees and briefly noticed some ketchup stain on the eyelet-designed garment. My black Mary Jane shoes were spotless though and my white socks looked like they were more than ready to retire. Cherubs don't wear dresses; they are forever wearing nappies and holding bows and arrows, I thought to myself.

"No, I look like a walking doll," I pouted, crossed my arms on my chest and she laughed, even her laughter sounded beautiful – lush, creamy, vibrant – like caramel and cream and lovely music all rolled into one.

"You prefer to look like a walking doll than a cherub?" she asked, her perfectly shaped dark brown eyebrows arched, her full rogued lips curved into an infectious smile.

"Please buy me one, Mama, or maybe you can tell Papa to buy one for me?" I tugged at her dress. I had wanted to have a walking doll and had repeatedly asked for one on numerous occasions but because it was an expensive toy, she was never able to buy one. Of course it disappointed me that Mama always had an excuse not to buy it, but I knew that if I kept on nagging her, she would eventually give in.

She shifted in her position and looked straight ahead, "I'll get you one when I make extra money at work, that's a promise. Now, sit still and look outside the carriage, look at those balloons, aren't they pretty? Do you want one?" she pointed at a man carrying a mushroom of balloons. Her voice had gone taut and her brow had furrowed. I instinctively allowed her to train my attention to the balloon vendor and the colorful display caught my breath.

"I want a balloon! Balloon! Balloon!" I screamed as I jumped up and down, surprising the horse and causing our carriage to jerk. Well, if I can't have a walking doll now, then I'm pretty sure I can have a balloon at least. Anna grabbed and pulled me onto her lap, her arms firmly wrapped around my little body. I loved Anna. I loved her protective nature. I have always felt safe when she had her arms around me. I have always felt protected whenever she was around.

***

Chapter 2

Anna was a great dancer. She had long, beautifully shaped legs that shimmered under the swirling disco lights. I knew this because I saw her dancing on a ledge one evening and she was wearing a tiny red sequined bikini that displayed her supple, ivory skin. She was wearing knee-high boots and there she was, right in the middle of the ledge along with other women on either side of her and all of them were wearing bikinis and stilettos and boots, each one of them fully made up. I stood there, behind a semi-parted curtain, as I watched my mother gyrate gracefully to the tune of Kim Carnes' Bette Davis Eyes. Below the ledge were tables and chairs occupied by many men, some were watching the ladies on the ledge intently, others were drinking beer merrily and there were others still who were obviously enjoying the show too much they couldn't help but clap their hands up in the air and scream above their lungs. The lewd show, the men leering at the dancing women on the ledge and the swirling air in the musty club that reeked of cigarette smoke and alcohol told me this is a scene that I was not supposed to be watching, but I could not walk away from it.

"Come on! Remove that top! We wanna see more than just dancing, we want a show!" an old, beer-bellied man yelled from a corner while his companions back-slapped him and laughed. The crowd was a heavy mix of dirty old men, middle-aged husbands who probably were too bored with the idea of coming home early to their wives, young men no more than thirty years old who were obviously hoping to spend the night in the warm company of a sexually experienced woman. It didn't take a lot of cajoling from the male audience for it wasn't too long before a piece of stringed garment flew from across the room and landed on one of the beer-laden tables. I looked at the direction where it came from and I saw that one of the ladies had taken her bra off. Her big, perky breasts jiggled with every move she made, her hips swayed with the beat of the music and judging from her blank and spaced-out facial expression, she was high on pot. The crowd grew even more boisterous and some of the men started screaming for more. Another bra flew off, and then another, and another resulting to more jeers, catcalls and applauses. Anna and a few other girls still had theirs on and I held my breath as I watched Anna's every move in anticipation. I saw her raise her left arm above her head and turn her back on the crowd, hips gyrating to the pulsating music. Her right hand came up to her back, and touched the edge of the string that tied her bikini in place. I knew for a fact, having watched her try on different bikinis at home, that one tug at that string and everything will fall off. I watched intently, my young mind growing more confused with each passing second as I tried to absorb the scene before me. What was the dancing and stripping for? She was supposed to be manning the cash register. She told me that's what she does here. Time seemed to have stood still for a moment until I felt my small body being lifted up in the air as a pair of hands slid under my arms.

"What are you doing there? You should be sleeping. Come on; let's go back to your room. Little girls should not be staying up so late or you will never grow tall," Auntie Solita scolded gently.

"Auntie, I want to watch Mama dance, please," I begged.

The woman twirled me around so that our faces met and simply said, "It's not good for young children like you to watch that show." She walked me back to our room and stayed until I fell asleep, only to be roused back by whispering voices.

"She was behind the curtain watching you and the girls."

"Damn! What had she seen?"

"A sea of breasts."

"Damn! Did she see me strip?"

"I caught her just in time."

"I'll see the old lady on the other side of town tomorrow. She was recommended by Mark. He said she's good with children." Mark was the club manager. He was a nice looking guy who spoke with a lisp and walked around with his hips sashaying gracefully. He also doubled as choreographer, it was fun to watch him coach the girls how to do perfect turns and body swings. Anna was the only club employee who had a child stay in with her in her quarters which she shared with Auntie Solita, which caused the envy of a lot of the girls who had children of their own and started a controversy amongst the group. Mark was accused of playing favorites and some of the ladies were not too discreet in showing their dislike for Anna. Eventually, Mark decided to help Anna look for someone who would be willing to take me in and care for me while Anna worked in the club. He was desperate to keep the peace among the ladies and Anna was desperate to keep her job.

"Anna, your daughter is a smart girl. She will find out eventually and there is nothing you can do about it. Just tell her the truth."

"No. I am not ready yet."

Auntie Solita sighed in resignation, "When will you ever be?"

The next day, Anna took me on a trip to a nearby village that was lined with wooden homes and bamboo trees. When we got there, children were playing out on the unpaved streets and there were groups of men and women in every corner, I noticed one group was playing cards and from a short distance, another group huddled together talking.

I was introduced to my new nanny, an old lady whose face I could no longer recall. Time has a way of snatching away some of my memories, relegating them to an unreachable corner of my mind.

Going back, my nanny shared her home with her husband, her daughter, son-in-law and grandchildren. Her grandchildren were older than me, I remember there were two boys and two girls and the boys promised to give me a ride on their cow the next day. The old lady's son-in-law and eldest grandson plowed the rice fields that lay beyond the small village, they were farmers; hence they owned a cow. I called the old lady "Lola", which meant "grandmother". Lola seemed to like me but she had other odd jobs aside from being my nanny, she was always not around and I would be left in the company of her grandchildren or her daughter, or whoever was at home. I didn't really care about who looked after me, anyway. I was too young to notice and to complain about such matters. I stayed with this family for quite a while. I was left in their care long enough for me to learn how to hold a penis and put it inside my mouth.

***

Chapter 3

    I would like to believe that Anna did her best to shield me from life's harsh realities. She hired one nanny after the other to look after me because she had to earn money for us to survive. She could not take care of me the way normal mothers took care of their children, especially when the one man whom she was expecting to support us is not stepping up to the plate. It was also convenient for her to have me safely tucked away somewhere else because it gives her a sense of freedom from having to constantly hide the truth from me. Anna didn't want me to know that she was a stripper because even from the start when I have already learned to ask questions, she told me she was a cashier. Perhaps, Anna thought it was best for me to know so little. Maybe, just maybe, she thought lying to me about the true nature of her job would protect my young mind from some form of corruption. Maybe because in this young girl's eyes, Anna was the epitome of beauty, strength of character and moral standards. Perhaps these are the reasons she lied, Anna didn't want my impression of her to be tainted. But then, she forgot one universal truth – that life has a funny way of bringing out the skeletons in everyone's closets eventually for all to see.

Unfortunately, Anna's intentions, no matter how good, only exposed me even more to life's cruelty.

I don't know how old I was - maybe four or five, just around that age- when it happened. I was playing upstairs by my lonesome self when one of the grandsons arrived.

"What are you doing there? Where is everyone?" he asked.

"Uh, outside. I don't know." I replied, barely looking up. I could see his feet firmly rooted on the bamboo floor, dry soil clung in between his toes and he smelled of dried sweat and sun. He just stood there and I briefly wondered why he wasn't leaving. I looked up and saw him staring at me. His hands were fumbling on the front of his jeans and his shirt was raised halfway his torso, exposing sun-burnt stomach and lower rib cage. I was rooted to my spot, staring back at him, not knowing that I was in imminent danger.

He then pulled his jeans down, just enough to let his penis out and he asked, "Do you know what this is?"

I shook my head.

"Come, touch it."

I shook my head and backed away, I didn't want to touch it, it looked scary! "It's a snake." I announced and he laughed.

"Yes, it's a snake, but it is a friendly snake. If you kiss it, it won't hurt you. Come, touch it gently and then kiss it."

"No, I don't want to. I'll tell your Lola you're letting me kiss a snake!" I stomped my foot and crossed my arms on my chest, triggering his anger. He bolted to a kneeling position and yanked me down on the bamboo floor; the nails that held the bamboo slats in place scraped the skin on my knees. He grabbed my arm and a shooting pain coursed through my shoulder at the impact. He held my wrist tightly and pulled my hand against his throbbing penis, my palm felt the heat of the shaft that he had been flailing to my face.

"Touch it!" he hissed. His voice sounded like thunder to my ears and when I looked up to search his face for a sign that all of it was just a joke, my eyes were met with a pair of chillingly dark, manic and angry pools. For the first time, I felt really terrified.

"I said touch it! You stubborn child!" he barked. I yanked on his penis instinctively as I felt panic and fear attack my senses. I wanted to run, I wanted to hide, I wanted to scream. I wanted to be transported into another place and time. But I was there, on my knees, in front of a teenaged boy who saw me as an easy target to relieve of his carnal craving.

"Don't yank, Jesus! Just, be gentle! No, no, not like that. Fuck, your mother is a star prostitute and you don't even know how to hold a penis? Learn from her! I heard she's good, just expensive!"

I started crying. I wasn't sure if I was crying because of the things he said or because I felt revolted at what he was making me do to his penis. I begged him to stop and let me go, but he was too consumed by his need that he didn't think twice about inflicting pain on a little child.

"Fuck you, little twat! Stop crying! Stop! Oh, I know what will make you stop, here, put this inside your mouth," he ordered as he yanked my head down to his groin, he gripped on my hair and started pushing and pulling on it to guide me. "Stick it in your mouth! Don't you bite it or I'll chop your head off!" he warned.

It was a warm summer day. The sky was clear outside and I could hear the faint rustling of bamboo leaves as the summer breeze brushed them. The air smelled of sun-dried leaves, Sampaguita flowers in bloom and cut hay. It would have been one of those lovely summer days when one's senses would easily be drawn to the beauty of the tropics, but the young man's stench of sweat, body odor and stale breath blowing on my little face spoilt it all. From a distance, I could hear a dog barking and an infant crying. I silently prayed for Lola to appear on the doorway, or someone, anyone. I willed for another human being to come and rescue me, but I was disappointed.

That night, I stared at the ceiling as I lay on my back alongside the other children, sleep eluded me. Instinctively, I knew that something in me had died. From the deep recesses of my innocent mind, I knew that I was violated and abused but I was warned not to tell or Anna and I will be killed. At such a young age, I had known how it felt to feel alone, desolate, confused and empty inside. A certain feeling of deep sadness hung over my head and for the first time, I wished we had a better life.

Unable to sleep and shake off the memories of what happened that day, I shifted to my side in the hopes of falling into a dreamless sleep should I change position. The moment I shifted, there he was staring at me. Two children lay asleep between us giving me a momentary sense of safety but his eyes penetrated through me, wrapping my heart in absolute dread. I stared back, caught between shifting into another position and pretending not to see him, but he knew because slowly, he raised his index finger to his lips which were formed in a straight, stern line. It was a silent warning laced with a silent threat. And so I was hostaged.

***

Chapter 4

    I have always displayed a stubborn character even as a young child. I was never hesitant about expressing how I felt or what I thought. There were times when Anna would ask me to do something and I would tell her outright if I didn't want to do it, or if I wanted to then I would immediately respond. Auntie Solita often said that I am Anna's small version – stubborn, headstrong and unbending. Anna would acknowledge this half-heartedly, throwing Aunt Solita dagger looks sometimes. While Anna was everything I wished I would become someday, it was the opposite for my mother. "Do I look like Anna, Auntie Solita?" I would ask the woman who was the only next of kin I thought we had. But Auntie Solita knew better than to raise my hopes up, she knew that while there was a resemblance between Anna and I, my father's features dominated my looks. I had fair skin, but not as fair and creamy as Anna's, my hair was thin and straight, my nose a little round and I had my father's dark-colored eyes. "You are beautiful in your own skin, little darling," she would gently say.

Auntie Solita was Anna's bestfriend, as I would later come to understand. They were an inseparable duo, sharing dreams, hopes, homes, meals and weed. She was a nice woman whose looks were a stark contrast to Anna's. She had dark, straight hair that fell like curtains down to her slim waist. Her skin was a beautiful tan, like that of the famous actress *Nora Aunor's and she was a lot shorter than Anna, who stood at 5 feet 5 inches. Auntie Solita possessed an easy, charming smile, the kind of smile that wraps the heart with warmth on a cold December morning. Whenever Anna would be angry at me for being disobedient or for not wanting to eat my vegetables, I would run to Auntie Solita for comfort. She would shoo Anna away and take me into her arms where I would cry my little heart out.

"Hush now, you have to eat your veggies, they're good for you," she would coo next to my ear.

"I hate vegetables, Auntie," I'd sob and she would rock me back and forth while caressing the top of my head. I despised squash, eggplant and okra so much I would rather suffer the ire of my parents than eat any of it, but they were a staple meal for our odd family because they were the only food we could afford to buy on most days. I don't really remember how those episodes ended. Maybe sometimes they were able to knock some sense into my stubborn little head and I ate my vegetables, but I bet most of the time they failed at it because Anna sometimes fed me with rice mixed in water and sugar. But, I remember how good it was to have someone to run to for comfort whenever Anna and I would have disagreements. Auntie Solita provided a shelter that allowed me to be who I was and chided my mother for wanting me to be different.

"She is your daughter. What do you expect?" she would often ask Anna.

"That's the point, she is my daughter and I don't want her to be like me. Look where my stubbornness had taken me," Anna would point out.

"Anna, she won't end up the way you did. You are far too much of a better mother than that. Don't be so hard on yourself; your daughter has a bright future because you will be there to guide her."

"I hope so… I just… I just don't want her to end up not having any choice left someday."

I never really understood what Anna meant whenever she would say that until much later. However, thinking about it now, Anna did have a choice if only she would lower her pride. She could go back home to my grandfather and rebuild our lives back in our charmingly idyllic hometown. Perhaps, it was also one of the reasons Anna put such a high premium on obedience – she wanted me to be an obedient child, always ready to do as she says, abide by her rules, follow her advice… But then again, I wasn't wired for any of that as well, especially where Anna is concerned. I could not understand why but it was far too easy for me to disobey her most of the time than otherwise.

Sadly, it wasn't Anna nor Auntie Solita who taught me the value of obedience. It was that boy who walked in on me one summer day when I was alone and saw an opportunity to shamelessly molest me.

Well, my initiation - like most - taught me a few valuable things but the most important of them all is that it is best to follow orders if I did not want to get hurt. Oh, and the sooner I did as instructed, the sooner my ordeal will end. So I learned how to be malleable when the situation called for it.

I have little recollection of how often it happened or of how many times more, I was too young to even know how to count my fingers. But it happened every now and then whenever I would be left alone in his care or whenever he saw a chance to lock us up together in a room. It happened long enough for me to learn how to give a teenaged boy decent blowjobs. Rule of thumb: Make sure you learn how to open your mouth enough to avoid grazing his penis with your teeth. Or else, I'd get a stinging slap on the face.

***

Chapter 5

I don't know what made Anna decide to terminate the old lady from her job as my nanny. Did she find out about the abuse? I guess that is a question I will never find the answer to. All I know is that Anna picked me up one day and brought me to the city. She said it was a special day because it was my birthday.

"What's a birthday, Mama?" I asked as I hopped and walked to fall into step with her. Geez, she had such long legs I could barely keep up, she held on to my right hand and almost dragged me as she strode along.

"It's the anniversary of the day you were born," she replied.

"How was I born?" I asked again.

"I gave birth to you. You grew inside my stomach and when you became big and heavy enough for my stomach to contain, I had to find a midwife to help you out," she explained.

I stared straight ahead as we traversed a rocky, dusty, sun-dried road and mulled over what she said. So, that's the reason why one of Lola's neighbors had such big tummy, there was a child growing inside!

"Is that how people are born?"

"Yes, first they grow in their mothers' tummies and then they are pushed out and become babies. And then they grow up because they eat vegetables. You are six now, but look at you, you're so skinny and small. You should start eating more vegetables."

I still hated vegetables. And being six didn't mean much to me.

"What's a midwife?" I asked again, hoping that my question would distract her from remembering to feed me vegetables tonight.

She briefly explained what a midwife is and it sounded like a profession that I wouldn't want to have anything to do with. I abhorred any job that required looking or holding blood, human parts and human waste that was why whenever Anna would say, "You will be one of the finest nurses this country will ever produce," I'd stomp my feet, cross my arms on my chest, pout and say, "But I want to be a teacher!"

After what seemed like an eternity of walking, we finally reached the end of the rocky road and stood on the side of a paved highway. Anna waved her right arm to flag down passing utility vehicles. Judging from the way the sun was shining, it was mid-morning and judging from Anna's attire which consisted of denim jeans, a white sleeveless top and sneakers, it looked like we were on our way to the city.

"Where are we going, Mama?"

"We are going to see your Godfather. And then we are going to visit the Grotto. Happy birthday, Darling," she replied as she stopped walking to scoop me up in her arms and kiss my cheek.

My Godfather owned a shop in the city. I don't exactly know what the shop's services offered but there were racks and racks of television sets. We didn't have a TV at Anna's nor did Lola's family have one. All Lola had was an old red transistor radio that boomed overhead every night before everyone fell asleep. Lola would hush us to settle down after dinner and she would switch on the radio just in time for a radio play I have come to learn as "Si Matar". The radio would crackle and hiss every night and I barely understood what the voices were saying, but what stuck with me was the eerie sound one of the characters made. I would crawl under my blankets and try to shut the noise out, I feared Si Matar. It sounded like a horror program.

Visiting my Godfather was a treat, he would give me money, candies and he would allow me to sit in front of one of the big TV sets and watch whatever program was on. He was a fair-skinned man, to my recollection, who had a mustache, straight cropped hair, a thin frame that was always slouched on his chair. He was always working on television parts, his table was always laden with screws, black boxes with circuits, tools and wires. I loved my Godfather for his kindness and even though I didn't get to see him often, I knew that he cared for me and Anna.

"How is… Uhm… Frank?" I overheard him ask Anna.

"Who can tell? He hasn't written in months. He hasn't sent any money. I went back to work." Anna replied with a sigh.

"At the club?" Godfather momentarily looked up from what he was doing to direct his question at Anna. Beads of sweat formed on his forehead and trickled on the side of his jaw. Anna was fanning herself with a piece of cardboard she had seen lying around. The air was humid, thick and heavy and Godfather's employees were predicting a heavy downpour soon.

"It's the only job I will probably ever be good at," Anna laughed in between words, revealing a perfectly white set of teeth and thin lines on her forehead. She can work here, I thought to myself, and then I can watch TV everyday.

My Godfather clucked his tongue and shook his head, "Find a man who will marry you, Anna."

"Sure. When you find a man who would take me and accept my daughter, let me know and I will sign the papers in a heartbeat," Anna replied a bit haughtily.

***

Chapter 6

Frank is my father. I never saw much of him, he was always away and Anna told me that the reason for his being away too often was that he worked overseas. She said that Frank wanted to send me to the best school in the city and he was working hard to save up for my school fees.

"Your Papa loves you, he wants the best for you," she would always tell me. Anna had nothing else but good things to say about him and I accepted that although the few times Frank would be home, I never felt that he was interested in me.

He would be with us few and far between, and on those times I would see him as an intimidating fixture inside our cramped-up apartment. He never said anything to me, but I felt that I had to avoid him most of the time just in case he would find something to be angry about. I would also put on my best behavior, taking extra care to be obedient, courteous and less inquisitive. Frank scared me. He had in him a negative kind of vibe that even a child like me could sense.

Frank was always angry about something. He would raise his voice and bark orders at Anna, who meekly did as she was told. Her spunk, devil-may-care attitude would fly out of the window and she would turn into the most obedient person you'll ever see. But Anna loved having Frank around. She loved it too much she would seem to forget that I existed.

    I remember waking up one morning to the sight of Frank and Anna's near-naked bodies on the floor, a thin mattress protecting their backs from the cold concrete floor. Frank had his hands inside Anna's lacy panties and I could see Anna's dark brown bushy pubic hair through the flimsy garment. Frank probably arrived while I was asleep because I was surprised to find him there. With trepidation, I crawled out of bed and stood above their sleeping heads. My stomach was grumbling, I wanted to wake Anna up so she could give me something to eat but I was instinctively afraid it would upset Frank. I padded towards the dining table to look for food; Anna probably cooked something before she slept and she always had food ready every morning anyway – or at least whenever Frank was not around. I tiptoed around the borderless square space we called "apartment" and reached the table in less than ten steps. There were a few empty bottles of beer, a saucer that contained yellow liquid stuff which smelled like vinegar, empty clear plastic wrappers with morsels of pork cracklings, an ashtray that was brimming with cigarette butts and a couple of half-empty glasses. They had obviously been drinking. I stuck my index finger inside one of the clear plastics, swiped it around to collect some morsel and licked it. My stomach growled so loud that I heard the noise travel up to my ears. I glanced at the two sprawled bodies on the floor, willing the lighter skinned one to wake up, but none of them stirred. I stood in the middle of the room for what seemed like eternity, not knowing what to do to quell my hunger, until I had a light bulb moment.

I ran to a corner and quietly pulled off the lid on a tin can that held our rice reserve, stretched my skinny arm and dug through the rice until my hands felt a mound. Beneath the rice lay a canistel (also known as 'chesa'), an Asian fruit that Anna brought home for me just a few days ago. I pulled the yellow fruit out and lightly pressed on its skin, it had ripened, just as Anna had promised. It was my first time to eat the fruit and Anna had told me that it's one of her favorite fruits.

After eating my breakfast of canistel and beer-laced water from one of the glasses on the table, I decided to skip outside and play with the neighborhood children. It wasn't long before my playmates' mothers started calling each child in, apparently it was already time for lunch. I hopped my way back to the apartment but Frank and Anna were still fast asleep. Not knowing what to do, I went back outside and knocked on one of the doors.

"My Mama and Papa are still sleeping," I told the lady that greeted me at the door.

"Oh, you poor child. Come inside and eat with us," she said as she took my arm and gently pulled me in.

"My Mama said it is bad to eat at someone else's house, can I just sit here instead?" I inquired.

The lady's expression softened even more and patted my head. "It's okay, I won't tell her you ate here. Come," she invited.

I was hungry and she said she won't tell so I was more than happy to accept the invitation.

When I came home later, Frank and Anna were already awake and fully dressed.

"Where have you been?" Frank boomed across the room.

"I played with the neighbor's kids, Papa," I softly answered.

"You went out without telling your mother? Look at you, you're filthy!"

Anna grabbed me by the hand and started peeling my clothes off as she whispered, "I told you not to upset your father when he's home. Be a good girl and stop running around outside! Stay put inside the house, you hear me?"

"Mama, you were sleeping," I reasoned.

"Ssshh!!!" she hissed strongly enough for me to know it was time to completely shut up.

She gave me a bath, scrubbing my feet with a bathroom scrubber too quickly and too harshly it stung my skin. She soaped me and then doused water to wash the suds off. She did it too mechanically and too hurriedly that I could barely gulp in air in between each douse. After drying me off with a towel, she pulled out a pair of shorts and a shirt from a drawer and instructed me to wear them, which I quietly did, and then she sat me on the dining chair and set food in front of me.

"Eat and then take a nap," she whispered.

I had already eaten, but I could not tell her that. I tried to force the food down my throat but my stomach was too full, too heavy and too unwilling to take any more in. I must have been trying to consume the food before me for too long already that Frank noticed.

"You're not done with your meal yet?" he asked.

I felt panic rise to my throat and instinctively shoved a spoonful inside my mouth. Even my esophagus could not take any more in, I gagged. I gagged too loudly, loud enough for Frank to hear and to earn his ire.

"What's the matter with you? You don't like the food? You don't want to eat? Don't you dare throw up or I'll spank you!" he warned.

It felt bad enough to force food in when you're already too full to even chew anything else, but it felt even worse to hear your own father tell you that he will spank you if you threw up. I felt like throwing up. The fear mixed with the feeling of fullness made my stomach churn, I felt sour liquid rise up my throat and I tried to swallow it, God knows I tried, but I failed.

There was vomit on the floor and Anna ran to get the cleaning supplies. Frank walked up to me and started berating me. I don't remember anything he said, but I remember being punished by kneeling on a salt-laden corner with my arms stretched out on my sides for what seemed like forever.

I never ate at my neighbor's house again after that. But whenever Frank and Anna would sleep in and forget about preparing food for me to eat when I woke up, I would sneak outside and eat sand. Sand didn't make me feel full, but it took away the hunger pangs.

***

Chapter 7

Shortly before I turned seven, Anna taught me how to write my name. She was so proud of how quickly I picked up on my alphabets; she even bought a mini blackboard for me to scribble on. I wanted colored chalks but she said she could only afford the white ones, so I abandoned the thought of drawing flowers and houses and stick figures, concentrating instead on learning how to write my big and small ABC's. Anna showed my writings to Auntie Solita, who announced that I was ready for school.

"I know, she's almost seven, she can start school next term," Anna answered in the affirmative. The thought of going to school excited me that I could barely stop nagging Anna about it.

"How soon is next term, Mama? I want to go to school already," I would ask her every morning as soon as I woke up, every night before she would tuck me in and in between whenever I would remember about it.

"Soon. Don't worry, you will be in school soon," she would assure me. She probably ran out of patience eventually because I just could not help myself from nagging her about going to school, so one morning she woke me up early, got me dressed and took me to a nearby school.

We met with a kind lady about Anna's age and they talked in a corner while I explored the classroom, taking in the smell of pencil erasers, Manila paper, glue and text books. I was impressed with the big blackboard that almost covered one of the four walls. There were lots of chairs, neatly arranged in three rows facing the big blackboard. One chair could sit three children. I ran my tiny hands across the chairs, feeling the wood beneath my palm, skimmed through the text books neatly arranged in a corner shelf and wrote ABC on the blackboard using a small piece of chalk I found on the small chalk container by the teacher's table. I was so excited.

"Is this going to be my school, Mama?" I asked Anna who turned to me with a smile and an affirmative nod.

"Is she going to be my teacher?" I asked again. The lady smiled at me and said something, but I didn't quite catch what she said so I just shrugged my shoulder and went back to scribbling on the blackboard. It wasn't long before we bid her our goodbyes.

"When am I going to start school?" I asked Anna.

She had a funny look on her face, her lips were pursed, her expression was taut and her eyes looked angry and sad at the same time. She didn't answer me and I decided to let it go. I wondered briefly what she was thinking, but forgot all about it as soon as we saw an ice cream vendor around the bend on our way out of the school gate.

***

Chapter 8

The Grotto was an imposing statue of the Virgin Mary which stood on top of a hill in a sleepy town north of where we lived. Anna would take me there every year as part of my birthday celebration. She would guide me along the one hundred flight of stairs that was the only way to reach the foot of the statue and for me, it was the most punishing way to celebrate any birthday. But I was not allowed to complain for fear of being punished even more severely. Anna warned me that the Virgin Mary could read my thoughts and hear every word every other human being on this planet ever uttered and children who complained about coming up to the Grotto would be punished by getting polio, apparently a type of illness that rendered one who ever contracted it to become disabled for life.

"You won't be able to walk anymore for the rest of your life, do you want that?" she would ask me towards the end of her story about how the Virgin Mary expressed her disappointment.

So I would climb up the stairs with her and not once complain about how the whole exercise rendered me almost disabled already. Once on top, we would stand still in front of the imposing statue and pray. Well, Anna prayed. She prayed a whole lot longer than any person I knew, so I would run around and find things to keep me busy while she did her business of praying. After making the sign of the cross, she would then lay a bunch of Camias strewn into a ley on the statue's feet and then guide me back to the bottom of the stairs. Just below the hill, we would stop by one of the eateries and she would order food and soda, after which she would pull out a cigarette stick from her purse and light it up while staring out onto the expanse of land before us.

"Why do we pray, Mama?" I asked her on that particular trip.

"Because we ask for forgiveness for our sins, we seek guidance so that we will always do good and then we beseech Jesus for blessings," she answered in between cigarette puffs.

"Is it my birthday today?" I asked again.

Anna simply looked at me and smiled. There was a particular sadness in her eyes and her smile didn't quite reach those beautiful amber-colored pools. I could not understand it, but I felt it. There was something unmistakably different about today and by the way she answered or did not answer my question told me that it wasn't my birthday. I looked at the plastic bag that she had been clutching since we left home and I saw that it contained some of my clothes.

"Hey, those are my clothes!" I pointed inside the plastic bag.

"I am taking you to your Grandmother's house, you like staying there don't you?" she said. Ah, there was also a tinge of sadness in her voice.

"Really, Mama? Yes! I like staying there. You know Lolo and I jog every morning and we collect macopa and mabolo fruits from the neighbors' trees. And Lolo has this huge santol tree and a pet monkey. And Lola likes to cook so much food, too, Mama. She cooks delicious food all the time," I babbled on excitedly not quite knowing that my life was about to take a sharp turn.

She took me to Frank's parents and told me I will be staying there for awhile. I loved staying at my grandparents' house. It's a big 1970's style two story home that had a large living room, a family room, a dining area with an eight-seater dining table, a large kitchen area where my grandmother cooked wonderful meals as well as a spacious yard shaded by my grandfather's fruit-bearing trees. It was a stark contrast to Anna's apartment, which was cramped and bare. But the apartment was home to me and after a few days, I started missing Anna. I started wondering when she was coming back. I would stand by the gate outside and look out on the street, hoping to catch a glimpse of Anna. But as each dusk overtook the light of day, I would return inside the house with a heavy heart for Anna never came. There was not a day that I did not hope to see her knocking on the door to take me home with her and there was not a moment that I did not miss her. It was just like that. Not a word. Not a warning. She just disappeared from my life.

Looking back, Anna was not the ideal mother every child would want to have, but she was my mother and she loved me the best way she could. When times were tough, she would go up on the nightclub stage and dance while stripping herself bare for the jeering patrons to watch because it was the only way she could earn money to put food on our table. Deep in my heart I know she tried to be the best mother that I could ever have, but Anna can only stretch herself as far and bend her back only as low. It may not be the best by society's standards, but it was her best.

***

Chapter 9

I celebrated my seventh birthday in a house I was later taught to call 'home' where my new family lived. My new mother was Frank's legal wife, and what did I know? I had siblings! Four to be exact- 3 brothers and 1 sister. The eldest was older than me by about six years, followed by another brother who was older than me by about four years, then a big sister who was older than me by a year and then a little brother who was no more than three years old when I joined the family. My new mother was a beautiful woman who worked for the local government. She was a clerk of court. On weekdays, she would be at work from 8 in the morning until 5 in the afternoon and on weekends, she would be a typical mother – cooking, doing the laundry, ironing clothes, cleaning the house and putting her children to sleep for siesta. She was mild-mannered, she dressed in conservative clothes and she didn't smoke nor drank alcohol. She was a far cry from Anna who was a woman of the world. My new mother also gathered us, her children, every night around the altar to pray the Holy Rosary. On Sundays she would wake everyone up really early and get us all dressed in fancy clothes to attend Sunday mass. She was deeply religious. Her set of religious beliefs would totally blow Anna away, if all Anna knew and practiced was going to the Grotto and praying at random times. This woman – my new mother – prayed the Holy Rosary, the Novena, attended regular Sunday mass, weekly bible studies and her prayers, as she later taught me, were sequenced: First you praise God, then you thank Him for his blessings, then you ask for the atonement of your sins, and then ask for more blessings. Strictly in that order, or God will not hear your prayers.

She was also obsessively organized. Each of her children, including me, the new addition, had tasks to perform every weekend to help keep the house in order. She said all little girls should learn how to keep their surroundings neat and tidy, a practice that they must learn until they grow old enough to get married. "Otherwise your future mother-in-law will return you to me," she would quip.

I also discovered later that we have a rather large family. Everywhere we went, we were instructed to pay our respects to the elders by putting the back of their hand on our foreheads as a form of greeting and sign of respect. We regularly did rounds of visits to different relatives – cousins, uncles, grandparents of up to the third degree of affinity and consanguinity. It was hard for me to keep up with everyone's names, so I instead learned how to call all the older cousins "Kuya" (Big Brother) and "Ate" (Big Sister), and purposely omitted first names for Aunts and Uncles and Lolo and Lola.

For the first few months since my arrival, I felt like a little debutante being presented to the public. The only problem's that I was an unwelcomed debutante. My new mother would gather us all every weekend and we would troop to every relative for a "visit" and then I would be introduced.

"Who is that little girl?"

"That's Frank's daughter," my new mother would announce.

"Oh, that is his daughter from that prostitute?"

And my new mother would bob her head to confirm.

"She has light skin, she's a pretty little girl,"

"Her mother is prettier," my new mother would say.

"Oh, you better discipline that child lest she takes after her mother's character," our relatives would advise.

And again, my new mother would bob her head in agreement.

"Why did you want to add up to your headaches? Oh, bless your kind heart. When you die, you will surely go to heaven."

And once more, my new mother would bob her head.

In my mind, I was imagining that I was rolling my eyes, stomping my feet, crossing my arms on my chest and pouting in disagreement with the conversations going on above my head.

Needless to say, I suffered from discrimination from this new family's family. They would look at me and whisper among themselves, whispers that were loud enough for me to hear or piece together, "That's Frank's daughter from that stripper."

"Frank had a daughter from that bitch?"

"Why yes, she's looking at us right now. Hush..."

And there was one time I tried on a new dress that my new mother bought me, it was such a beautiful pink dress that flowed just about an inch down to my knees and its skirt was so soft it moved against the wind. My new mother asked me to walk around the living room so she could see me better and when I did, I was having so much fun wearing the dress that I walked around sashaying my hips playfully. My grandmother – my new mother's mother – exclaimed, "Stop walking like that!

Nice girls don't walk like sluts. Do you want to be like your mother?!"

This was when everything started to fall into place for me. This was when I realized why I never saw much of my own father when I was still with Anna. The realization that I am my father's daughter from another woman and the ripple effect of that fact hit me like an avalanche. More so is the realization that my mother earns money in exchange for sexual favors.

Anger, confusion, hate and all things spiteful started to take root in my heart. I started to question my very existence. I began to hate Anna and Frank, blamed them for giving me a life which, at an early age, I knew I did not deserve. I learned to envy other families and wished I had been born into a conventional family. My worldview drastically changed and I had become one angry, negatively and emotionally charged little human being.

Eventually, I realized too that I didn't want to be like my mother. I wanted to be my own person, to have my own dreams, set of beliefs and ideals. I desperately wanted to have my own set of values and principles that were polarized from Anna's. But I live in a place where the unschooled were taught by their mothers and their mothers' mothers that no fruit shall fall far from its tree.

And so I struggled. My youth struggled to break free from the stigma of being the daughter of a stripper and a home wrecker. I struggled to belong to a family that never needed nor wanted me in the first place. I struggled to make the people around me love and accept me. I struggled to crawl as far away as possible from the shadows of the woman who brought me out into this world.

***

Chapter 10

Shortly before my eighth birthday arrived, a nightmare that I was once so familiar with came back. Who would have thought that even in the supposed safety of your own home, you may not really still be safe? That danger lurks even when you thought that you're protected by the people you call family?

One of my half-siblings made me realize this ugly truth when he started abusing me. First, by himself and then sometimes with his friends. I became their human toy, they played with my privates and had me play with theirs. What started out as plain touching, fondling and caressing the first few times progressed to actual sex. I could not say that I did not like it, but I also could not say that I did. It was confusing for an eight year old to really understand how one should feel about things like that, after all I wasn't aware that I was already being violated. All I knew was that what they were doing to me was wrong because they did it whenever no elders were around and they made sure that the doors were locked all the time. Of course, I was warned not to tell, or there will be severe consequences.

However, I became aware of my own sexuality. I knew that if someone touched a certain part of my vagina, it would send electrifying pleasures all over my body. And if I stuck a finger inside, there is a delicious sensation that would travel up to my tummy and make me feel good. If I hung my feet up while I was being penetrated, it would feel slightly even better than when I didn't. And it pleased my rapist, too and when it pleased him it meant that playtime would end much sooner so then I can finally go back to playing with my hand-me-down Barbie doll. That was a lot better than being locked up in a room and playing with the boys' penises.

Like I said, it was confusing. The sensations playtime with the boys evoked messed up with my head so much most of the time. I didn't understand why I felt guilty, revolted, dirty, good, "womanly" (womanly is not a feeling that an eight year old should be having about herself!), wanted, needed and violated all at the same freakin' time.

And so, playtime – sometimes with just my half-sibling and sometimes with his friends – went on until I was around eleven years old. By that time I already knew what it all was – rape. I realized I was already being raped when I first encountered the word on the six o'clock news. They reported a child who was raped by a neighbor and I asked my new mother's mother what that meant. The old woman explained what rape was and it felt like I was punched in the gut to realize that I am a rape victim. I stared at my new grandmother and thought about telling her what was happening to me but fear gripped me. Would she believe me? How would she feel about her grandson raping a child? She looked so frail and weak, what if something happened to her and the whole family blamed me? What if it reached Papa and suffered a heart attack or worse, went amok and killed his own son? Then the whole family would hate me forever and I will end up not having anyone to call 'family' anymore…

I couldn't. I needed to belong. I needed to have a family. I was much too young to support myself.

***

Chapter 11

By the time I was eleven or twelve, the rape had stopped. I don't know what made him stop, but it just did and I was relieved. But it had created a scar so deep into my soul that even I could not understand myself sometimes. I became even more rebellious. I was extremely disobedient, I lied a lot, I hated staying at home so I would often run away only to be found, brought back home, punished and ostracized by everyone for a few days. However, I was doing really well in school. I won awards for my writing, I was a creative student and on the outset, I looked like just any other normal kid – happy, playful, studious and respectful to my teachers. I graduated from grade school with flying colors. I was "Most Reliable Student" for keeping my classmates busy whenever the teacher would be out selling meat products to her co-teachers. Believe it or not, in public schools here, teachers have what they called 'sidelines', they would sell wares to other teachers such as meat products, candy products, Tupperware products, Avon products, real estate and insurance. They usually do all that during school hours and to keep their students from running around when they should be holding classes, the teacher would give the students something to do (read several pages of a textbook and answer the questions at the end of the story or transcribe the story on a notebook), appoint the Class President to make sure that the children did as told and the Class Secretary to keep tab of the noisy kids. Well, I was Class President.

Anyway, going back, I also graduated "Most Honorable Mention" which meant that I belonged to the Top Ten of our class. I was almost certain that my Father would be so proud of me for giving honor to his name. Well, I was mistaken.

On the morning of the graduation ceremonies, I found out that Papa did not come home the night before so I went to school to attend my graduation alone. About an hour or so later, Papa arrived with the school principal and my Class Adviser tapped my shoulder to let me know that Papa arrived. I smiled at her and thanked her for letting me know but before I could even finish my sentence, another teacher came up to her and whispered (again, loud enough for me to hear), "The School Principal finally arrived, with her boyfriend. What a shameless bitch, displaying her married boyfriend here!"

I think people should train themselves to whisper in such a way that nobody else would hear. I sat down on my chair and kept staring at the program I was holding. Should I also be ashamed for being the daughter of the principal's boyfriend?

When my name was finally called, I went up the stage, my back slouched and my head bowed down. I wanted dearly to puff my chest out, look ahead, smile and be proud of what I have accomplished, but Papa's presence just could not make me. Especially since he had remained rooted next to the principal from beginning to end, coming up next to me only for a photo op.

When I came home after the ceremonies, everyone else was there but it looked just like any other ordinary day. No special meal on the table, no congratulatory wishes, nothing. I was disappointed, sad and demoralized. "All the hard work for nothing?" I asked myself in despair. Not even Papa expressed how proud I made him or not.

I told my sister about how I felt that night before we went to bed, she looked at me and condescendingly replied, "Oh sure you're the first from this family to graduate with awards and to earn medals every year in school but don't you dare forget, you go to a cheap public school and we all go to a private school. Our subjects are much more difficult than yours. You wouldn't even make it to the best section if you attended the same school!"

My heart sank even further to a bottomless pit... A part of me hated Anna even more, but another part of me wished she was around...

***

Chapter 12

While I have this unquenchable feeling of hate for my own mother, there were still many nights when I cried myself to sleep because I missed her terribly. I miss the way she would do my hair to make me pretty. I miss putting talc powder on her body while she was asleep (and when she'd wake up and see herself in the mirror, she would just laugh at herself and then kiss me all over). I miss going to the Grotto with her on my birthdays. I miss listening to her sing her own version of Imelda Papin and Claire dela Fuente songs. I miss being able to reach out and touch her and whisper in wide-eyed wonder to her face, "Mama... Why are you so beautiful?", which delighted her so much she would reward me with butterfly kisses on my pudgy cheeks, my button nose, my eyelids, my forehead and finally my lips.

I just missed her so much too often that it hurt to not know where she was. Why did she give up on me? Did she realize that she didn't love me anymore? If she found out I was raped and that this new family I have didn't really love nor care for me, would she come charging down and demand that I be returned to her? I kept on hoping and praying for her to return and get me back and week after week, month after month, year after year something in me died a little because she never came.

Eventually, I stopped missing her. I stopped wondering about her and being worried about her safety. I found myself suspended between loving and hating her. And then, I started blaming her. I blamed her for every little and big thing that I suffered – the rape, being unaccepted into this family in which she threw me in without my permission, for not giving me a chance to have a say in her decision to give me up, for being treated unfairly by my new family, for failing Math in high school, for losing the drive to do good in school and so on and so forth. I just hated her so much that I started thinking, "Hey, if my own mother didn't love me enough to keep me, who else would?"

The thing is, pain changes people. Maybe not all, but it definitely changed me. The pain of being abandoned by Anna and being thrown into a world that looks at me as "that bitch's daughter" slowly crept unto my subconscious until it consumed me like a wildfire.

I began to hate myself, too and I started charging towards a self-destructive path. I stopped building dreams and working at reaching those dreams. I intentionally didn't work on my school assignments, I intentionally failed my subjects, I intentionally drove Papa nuts by bringing home a report card laden with red "F" marks in Math and Science, I started smoking and drinking, skipping classes and getting involved with boys. I also started having trust issues, insecurities and an overwhelming need to please the people around me except my family. Whenever the going got tough for me, I contemplated on committing suicide.

My early teenage years were the darkest, most turbulent times of my life. I was a ticking time bomb. No one understood what was going on inside my head. Even I could not fathom the depth of rage that was building up inside me, I just knew that I was running away from something that I could not quite put a finger to and it was sapping my youth's energy, diminishing my zest for life and clouding my judgment. There would be times when dying seemed like the easiest way out. I cut myself, tried to overdose on diet pills and pretty much became reckless.

My father, who resulted to violence most of the time because he didn't know any better, decided that I should quit school. He thought that perhaps being confined at home would straighten me out. For three years, I stayed home to oversee the house's upkeep, to cook meals, do the laundry and run errands. I felt like the equivalent of a housemaid and I hated Papa and Anna even more for it. I must admit that not being in school softened me up a bit and the quiet times at home, when everyone would be in school or at work, gave me the opportunity to think straight. The unquenchable need to escape fueled my desire to return to school. I realized that not being in school would only keep me strapped to this family forever.

So, I talked to him and told him that I wanted to go back to school. He made me promise to do better this time and warned me that it was my last chance. "If you mess this up one more time, you're never going back again," he said. The following school year, I earned my ticket to freedom from housekeeping and enrolled in a nearby high school.

Boy, did I do better than expected! I joined the school paper and ran for the Student Council. I perfected my exams; I burned the midnight oil and brought home bacon after freakin' bacon.

I finished High School at age nineteen. I was three years late, because people here finish high school at age sixteen. But I didn't care. Papa did not attend my graduation, nor did any of my siblings or new mother. But that's alright, I had grown calloused and numb to it already to take it personally (or so I thought!).

Papa did not send me to college. Gone was my childhood dream of becoming a teacher. I wanted to take up Political Science and pursue Law thereafter. But then, Papa said he had no money to support my studies and that if I really wanted to go to college, I would have to find a job to support myself through it. So I did. I found a job as a correspondent in a local newspaper company and took up AB Sociology in one of the mid-range universities in the city. Unlike many people I knew who worked to support themselves through school, the pressures of working and studying at the same time was too much for me to handle so when the time came for me to choose between school and work, I chose work and quit Uni. This is a decision that I would later on regret.

But before the regretting part, I enjoyed life as much as I could. Working to support myself meant being free from the clutches of my family, being free and finally having the power to leave home. I didn't really understand it but it seemed that being away from them became such a strong driving force in my life. It was like it was the only thing that I ever wanted.

And I did. I left home the moment the opportunity presented itself and did not return for fifteen years.

***

Chapter 13

Eventually, Papa found out that his own son raped me. Of course, he found out from me. When I left home, Papa tracked me down and because I lived so far away and was already employed and under contract, he could no longer take me back home with him. But he came down to where I lived to visit and talk to me. I am eternally grateful to whatever spirit possessed my father that day for in all the years that I have lived under the same roof with him, it was the only time he ever sat down with me in the same room and spoke to me like I was really his daughter.

"This is a nice place you have. Are you eating well here?" he asked.

"Yes, Papa. I think I gained about ten pounds since I came here," I smiled.

We sat on my kitchen table having coffee and since it was also the first time that I ever sat anywhere near my father (except during those times he was belting me or punishing me), I was able to take a closer look at his face... He had grown older, there were white hairs poking out of his head and the lines on his face had become deeper. His eyes looked older, more tired, kinder and less angry.

"Do you like it better here?" he broke into my reverie and I switched my attention to the delicate floral paintings on my coffee cup.

"Papa, this is home to me now. I've been here for six months already. I like it here, Papa. Please don't ask me to come back home. I don't want to live in that house ever again."

My father looked at me and saw that I was struggling to stifle the sobs. He tilted his head sideways and looked at me differently, like he was searching for something on my face- no, it was like he was seeing me for the very first time.

"Did something happen to you in that house that you're able to say that?"

I had no choice. It was my only chance to let my father know how much I have suffered in the hands of his son and how it had broken my person. It was also the only window of hope I'd seen for my father to see that he had failed me as a father and that it is not yet too late to forge a better father-daughter relationship. It was the only opportunity I have to make my father see that I am a damaged soul, and that is why I am what I am.

He cried, tears streamed down his cheeks like water that flowed from a river. We cried together and grieved for the innocence that I lost in the hands of the people who were supposed to help me protect it. We mourned for my shattered youth and my broken perception of the words 'family', 'love' and 'sex'. And we cried for the years we have lost to hate, bitterness and self-destruction. And then we thought of Anna and wondered where she could be now...

"Would you like to look for her?" Papa asked.

I stared at him for a long moment and considered my options. I took our empty coffee cups to the sink and washed them silently. My mind raced to various twists and turns – would I like to? Would I find her if I did? If I did, then what?

"If I did, then what?" I vocalized my thoughts too loudly my father nearly jumped on his seat.

"Then you would have your answers."

"I don't know, Papa. What good would it all do now?"

"She is your mother. I know that if she had a choice she wouldn't give you up. She loves you. Remember that time, when you were little, your Mom (my stepmother) and I tried to get you from her and she fought like a wildcat?"

Of course, how can I forget about that? I had been staying with Papa and his family without knowing they were his family because I was too young to understand the situation. I was probably staying there for a few days already when Anna arrived and Papa refused to let me out of the house. I was playing with my siblings and I heard screaming and yelling outside, so I looked. I saw Anna, she had on this nice white furry coat and she was crying while Papa was talking to her and he looked really angry. But I didn't care about what was going on, all I knew was that Anna was there and that it was time for me to go home. So I ran outside and went to Anna, who then grabbed me. I was wearing nothing but my panties and a sleeveless shirt, my feet were bare. She carried me to an awaiting vehicle just a few yards away and as soon as we were inside, the driver started the engine and off we went.

I smiled at the memory, "What really happened there?" I asked my father.

"Your Mom and I had been trying to convince her to give you up since you were a baby. When you were born, Anna chose to give birth to you through a local midwife. She was renting a place owned by one of your Mom's co-workers and they knew that she was my mistress. The night she went into labor, that co-worker of your Mom's came by to let your Mom know, so your Mom went there. When you came out of her womb, you were blue and you didn't cry immediately as most babies did. Your Mom, having had experienced giving birth and having worked in a birthing clinic when she was in college instantly knew there was something wrong, so she took you to the hospital. You had weak lungs, you were a blue baby."

"And because of that you felt Mom had the right to take me from Anna?"

"No, it wasn't like that. Your Mom fell in love with you. She wanted to have many daughters and we only had one so she thought it would be nice to have you for a daughter. Sweetheart, it also felt like it was the right thing to do, to raise you in a normal family setting."

"She got what she wanted eventually, but how come I never felt like she loves me?"

"She does. But I wasn't the kind of husband that motivated her enough to show her emotions. She loves each of you, equally, I am sure. But she was too wrapped up in finding ways to earn money to see the family through because I didn't have a job and I was irresponsible. Someday, you will understand why things are the way they are."

"Would you happen to know why Anna gave me up?"

"She couldn't send you to school. We have all of your birth records and we didn't want to give them to her when she asked us."

Birth records are requirements for enrolling a child in school. Anna couldn't get me enrolled because my father refused to give her access to those records and he had told Anna that if she really wanted to give me a better future, she had to give me up. Anna was hostaged into doing what she did, she had no choice. Aside from withholding my birth records, Papa refused to give any more child support and Anna, poor Anna, could not find any more stripping jobs that earned enough to support our needs. She had grown older and every year, new strippers would come in and steal the limelight from her because they were younger and fresher. I didn't know that competition could be that stiff even in prostitution.

***

Chapter 14

"When she first found out that she was pregnant with me, didn't she consider having me... Uhm... Aborted?" I asked after a while. I have always wondered about this. Anna knew that Papa was a married man and getting pregnant is not the wisest thing to let happen considering the circumstance.

"No. I never asked her to do it, too. We just knew that another mistake won't make our wrongdoings right. Not that we thought of you as a mistake, we just knew we had been irresponsible for not using contraceptives and we had to face the consequence of that."

Memories of an afternoon came flashing in my mind. I sat up on the bed to find pieces of clothing, bottles of alcohol, cigarette butts and what-nots strewn all over the floor. All the windows were closed and there was just Anna in the middle of the room, crying her heart out.

"Mama?" I called out softly. She turned and her eyes were red and puffy.

"Go back to sleep!" she sternly commanded, so I went back to bed and pretended to go back to sleep. I closed my eyes but from time to time I peered to see what she was doing. She was just crying bitterly and I wanted so much to run to her and comfort her but she wanted me to sleep, so I had lain there for what seemed like hours and silently watched her pour her heart out.

After a while, she went against the wall and started banging her tummy on it. It was the first time I noticed that she had a bulge in her stomach. Anna was pregnant! And she was banging the child inside her on the wall and I didn't understand what it was for. I told Papa about this piece of memory and I noticed that his jaw had tensed.

"I got her pregnant for a second time, but our relationship had taken its toll on me and I had reached a point where I didn't want to be in it any longer. She knew that and yet she still got herself pregnant. We fought all the time..."

"Yes, I knew that because there were times I would hear you arguing. I also remember that one time you shaved her head." I cut in.

"I didn't want her stripping anymore but she was too stubborn for her own good. So I cut her hair too short so that the club manager won't let her dance anymore."

"She worked to provide for our needs," I softly reasoned out.

"I know. But I was too blind to see that."

"What happened to the baby?" I asked, remembering that we were talking about a baby who was obviously my sibling. My real, full sibling.

"We lost the baby. She did not carry it to full term, its heart stopped beating inside your mother's womb."

The alcohol, sleepless nights, marijuana smoking and banging her tummy on the wall killed the baby and eventually, Anna's relationship with Papa. Well, their affair was a lost cause anyway so it would have died in the long run even if the baby had lived.

"Did you ever have doubts about me being your own flesh and blood?"

"What?" Papa did not expect that question and I also knew that it was the last question he would want to hear from me, but I just had to ask.

"I've always wondered about that, Papa. You've always been distant to me, sometimes I'd feel like you're angry at me for no reason, other times I'd feel like I'm not your daughter. There were a lot of times I doubted if you're my real father."

Papa turned to me and for a brief moment, I saw a pained look cross his eyes... Regret? Heartbreak?

"I will never be able to explain why, but to answer your question, no. I never doubted that you are my daughter. Look at you, you look like me," Papa attempted some sense of humor and I took that as a signal that the conversation had concluded.

"Excuse me? I look like Anna. You have a big nose," I replied and we both laughed.

For once, I knew how it felt to have a father.

***

Chapter 15

I have been so accustomed to abuse, having lived in abusive environments all my life, that I seem to get magnetized by it. At 22, I entered into a relationship which was emotionally, sexually and physically abusive. He was fifteen years my senior and had full custody of his three young children from his first marriage. I fell in love with the children, at first sight. How any mother could leave behind such beautiful and smart children was beyond me and perhaps, because of having known the pain of being abandoned by a parent, my heart immediately went out to them. On the day he introduced me to his children, the middle child came up to me and said, "Are you going to be our Mom? Our mom left us, would you please be our Mom now?" I looked at his chubby little face and into his puppy dog eyes and I was instantly won over.

While the children were a joy to have around, their father increasingly became a burden to constantly deal with. I could have gone out at the first sign of abuse, but I held on and I even held on tightly, putting the children's welfare before my own all the time. I knew it would break their heart if I left and then I would just be following Anna's footsteps.

Perhaps, too, a part of me had hoped that the man would change, or perhaps I believed him when he would repeatedly tell me that no other man would love and accept me the way he did.

Ours was a turbulent relationship, filled with economic strife because he didn't have a stable source of income. His financial status was putting more dents into his already shaky self-esteem and he took out his frustrations on me, which I accepted blindly, justifying his actions most of the time, telling myself that he loved me and he didn't mean to do any of it.

The abuse started shortly within six months of moving in with him, but I did not see it until many years later because it was so subtle and deceiving that I could have been looking at it through rose colored glasses. By the time I became aware of it, I was already deep into the relationship.

The more subtle signs came in the form of always wanting to be together, stating that he misses me terribly whenever we are apart. And then as the months passed, he became illogically jealous. He got jealous with people at work and questioned me about the depth of my relationship with them, he also closely monitored me, dropping me off to work and picking me up, demanding to be introduced to my colleagues as my "husband" and then asking me about my day at work, expecting me to tell him every tiny detail. Eventually, I was forced to leave my job as a journalist to keep the peace. By the second year, he already had control of my social media accounts, email accounts and blog by demanding to know my passwords; and he prohibited me from creating a PIN code on my mobile phone. Next, he controlled my beauty rituals, accusing me of going to the salon and putting on make-up or lotion because I was trying to impress another man. This was when it dawned on me that I'm in an unhealthy relationship and so, one evening, we sat down together face to face and I told him that I want out.

He calmly stood up, called each of the children and lined them up in front of me.

"She doesn't love me anymore. She doesn't want to be with us annmore. She wants to leave us," he announced. I was so shocked by his actions that I just sat there, firmly rooted on the living room couch and watched as each child started crying and begging me not to leave.

"See, that is what you will do to my children if you leave us now. Maybe even worse! They love you, they have learned to love you more than they ever loved their own mother. How could you do this to them?" he asked me pointedly as the youngest and only daughter clung to me like she was clinging on for dear life. Of course that made me change my mind about leaving. I did not have the heart to inflict such trauma to his children.

This scene was to repeat itself over and over in a span of three more years until when it didn't work anymore, he threatened to commit suicide. He wrote a suicide note, blaming me in the event of his untimely death, making me feel responsible for his decision to end his life. He kept a handwritten copy of the note on his files and for good measure, he typed it in a word document and saved it in his computer's hard drive. He also informed his eldest son about it, making the child promise that it will be opened only in the event that he dies of unnatural causes.

It was an axe that hung over my head for the rest of that sickening relationship. I was so scared of being blamed and every night whenever I would imagine myself getting out of it, I pictured the children's accusatory looks. More importantly, I pictured them being orphaned and how much that would break them. I felt so helpless, hopeless and depressed that I went on an eating binge as an outlet. He seemed to approve of it though because he supported my newfound vice by making sure the house is well-stocked with food. When one of his friends commented on how much weight I have gained, he tartly replied, "Oh, I'm purposely fattening her up to keep men away from her."

***

Chapter 16

Towards our seventh year together, I have ballooned horizontally that friends back home could not believe it was me standing in front of them. We made occasional trips for mini-reunions with my high school classmates and as an attempt to repair my relationship with my family. We put up a show every time we were in front of my father. On the outset, we looked like a little happy family but my stepmother could see right through the façade.

"Do you even realize how morbidly obese you are right now?" she asked me one day.

"I am?" I asked, pretending to be in denial. I knew I was, I could not even walk three hundred meters without panting for breath. At five feet two inches, I tipped the scale at 170 lbs. and going to fitting rooms to try on nice clothes was extremely mortifying and traumatizing.

"You know I've read somewhere that some people who develop bad eating habits may be using food as an escape from their problems," she said.

"I'm fine, Mom." I replied, looking for a way to escape the conversation.

"You know you can always come back if you want to. We are your family. Come home, come home sooner than later…"

That was one of the most poignant moments between me and my stepmother, to my recollection. I wanted to jump right into her arms and just cry my heart out, but I could not, there was a huge lump in my throat and a painful constriction in my chest that I was so afraid I would collapse at her feet. I could not even speak and all I did manage was a wry smile before I turned my back on her to make my way to the bathroom.

The months that followed were spiritually breaking. I have lost my sex drive and my boyfriend often made me feel guilty for not wanting to have sex all the time. Many times, he coerced me whenever he wanted to unload himself. He did not care if I was sleeping or was tired or was having my menstrual period, he would just go right on top of me and use me until he was satisfied. Sometimes, he would film us while we were having sex or he would demand that we mimic scenes from a pornographic movie, telling me that it is just role playing and that it would help boost our sexual relationship. After every sexual tryst, I would run into the bathroom and scrub myself over and over and over, feeling dirtier and shattered. I would only stop from scrubbing my body when my skin had turned red and raw. I also forced myself to barf and there were instances when I thought about pouring muriatic acid on my genitals.

Eventually, I devised schemes to escape sex by using the children. I slept in their room or would ask them to sleep with me in our room just so their father would not attempt to make advances. I also applied for a home-based job that allowed me to work at night and sleep during the day. All of this took a toll on all of us, I gained more weight, he lost even more control of himself and the children started to feel the tension. By the eighth year of my relationship with him, we were already getting physically violent with each other. It got to the point where an argument ensued and it ended up with me being pulled by the hair and slammed back and head first on the pavement. I stood up, got hold of a huge planter and threw it on his head. Fortunately, the planter was soft enough from having been just watered that it did not cause fatal injuries. However, it gave him an opportunity to still fight back. He turned to face me and I was so sure at that moment that it was the end for me. He dragged me inside the house, slapped me hard that I felt my tooth move and locked me up in our bedroom. I was forbidden to leave the house for many days thereafter.

That was the turning point for me. I knew that I had to get out no matter what, because staying would risk either my life or his life. Swallowing every ounce of self-preservation, I worked on making him believe that our recent fight made me realize that I want to make things better between us. I turned into this insatiable nymph and started treating him like a king, giving in to all of his wants and needs in and out of bed. I successfully kept the peace until he had become complacent enough to return my mobile phone and allow me to leave the house on my own. When he finally did, I knew I could not blow my chance to freedom.

I was so traumatized that I kept looking behind me, thinking he had me followed. When I was sure there was no one, I immediately rang up my father.

"Papa? Would you let me live with you for a few months until I got settled?" I asked. There were no preliminaries, there were no hello's nor how are you's. Only a deep sense of urgency that reverberated through the telephone lines.

"We have been waiting for you for a long time already. Come home, now."

My father met me at the terminal and if he was shocked, he did not show it, because I came home bringing nothing with me except the clothes and pair of flip flops I was wearing.

"Your sister left many clothes in her bedroom, see if anything fits you," he said simply.

***

Chapter 17

At 30, I'd thought I've already experienced it all. Child rape, domestic violence, domestic rape, emotional abuse... What else could I not have gone through? If I was halfway through my lifetime, I prayed everyday that the remaining half would be better. My eight year relationship thought me to be more observant of how men dealt with me, to always be vigilant for signs of an abusive behavior and to run as soon as I find any. It also thought me that threats are simply that – threats. Often empty and devices used as emotional traps. Should a man tell you he would commit suicide if you leave him, do not believe for even a single second. Or if he ever did, do not blame yourself because it was his choice to die and not yours. My ex-boyfriend is still very much alive to this day and I have taken every measure necessary to keep as much distance between us as possible.

I met my now ex-husband in my early thirties. He was sweet, affectionate in private, soft spoken and weak in character compared to me. It was a whirlwind romance that eventually resulted into a bitter separation. There were lessons learned from my marriage, but perhaps they are better shared in another book, another time. Anyway, on the night before my wedding day, my stepmother pulled me aside for a brief chat.

"Tomorrow, your life as a married woman will begin. Don't you think it is time to look for Anna?"

I was taken aback, I didn't expect her to bring the subject of Anna up. But this time, it was a welcome question.

"Will you give me your blessing?" I asked.

"Of course! Look for her, you have my blessing," she replied.

Looking for Anna was like looking for a needle in a haystack. Papa and Mom gave me enough information to use, last names and places mostly and bits and pieces of information that Anna had shared randomly with Papa about her roots. Apparently, Papa wasn't even sure if the name that Anna signed on my birth records was her real name.

"Prostitutes during that time, and I believe even now, used pseudonyms. They never revealed their true identities. So I am not sure if your mother trusted me enough. When we met, she introduced herself to me as Anna."

The advent of the internet had made the world an even smaller place. I typed the last name Papa had given me and several people came up on my search. One particular individual caught my interest, he had the same last name and the location was perfect – it was Anna's hometown. I quickly typed a message and sent it to the guy.

"Hi. I am looking for my mother. Her name is Anna. She left me when I was seven and I was wondering if you knew her because you have the same last name."

It didn't take more than three days before I received a reply.

"Call this number. She will be able to help you. Her name is Sarah, she is my sister. 97321459. Good luck!"

With trembling fingers, I dialed the number and a woman answered rather breathlessly, "Hello?"

"Hi... Is this Sarah?"

"Yes. Who is this?"

I introduced myself and told her my purpose for calling.

"Anna is my older sister. I didn't know she had a child. Do you have other siblings?"

My hand shook so hard that the telephone slipped from my palm landing on the floor with a loud kling-klang.

"Honey, I have an Aunt! Oh my God, I am talking to Anna's sister and she is my Aunt!" I hyperventilated to my husband as I stooped down to pick the phone up from the floor. My knees felt like jelly, my stomach was doing a somersault and my heart was pounding I could hear it in my ears.

I wanted to cry, I wanted to shout with glee, I wanted to celebrate, but I couldn't. It was Sarah that I found and not Anna. And it was Anna that I needed to find.

Sarah and I met in person three days later and for the first time in my life, I knew how it felt to look at someone and say, 'Oh my God, I look just like you!' and mean it. Sarah was an older version of myself, except that I had semi-wavy hair and she was curly. Her nose was more pointed than mine, but we had the same oval-shaped face, dark brown eyes and full lips. We also had the same skin tone and height. While I am unmistakably my father's daughter in looks, there was also a strong resemblance between Sarah and I. We talked for hours, but it wasn't enough. Shortly thereafter, we planned to take a trip together and spend a few days getting to know one another.

Sarah was my gateway to the past. She provided a door that opened into a world that I never knew existed – my heritage. She told me about her father, my grandfather, the man whose blood run through my veins. She told me about her memories of Anna, how stubborn she was, and how beautiful yet rebellious she had been. How they never heard from her again after she ran away from home when she was sixteen years old.

A part of me was sad to discover that I will never meet my Jewish grandfather ever because he had died when I was ten years old. Yet, I was happy to discover what the other half of me was made up of.

"You have your Grandfather's genes in you. You are smart and beautiful. He was a smart, gentle, educated and kind man. Make him proud." Aunt Sarah told me on the last leg of our trip. We were having coffee on a terrace overlooking the majestic mountains and city lights of Baguio.

I looked far ahead and took in the sights and sounds around me, such a beautiful place... It would have been a perfect backdrop for this beautiful, poignant moment in my life, if not for the one person that should be here, but wasn't.

A tear fell from my eyes as I thought of Anna and how much she's been missing. Aunt Sarah wiped the tear away with a tissue paper and cupped my face with her hands, she brought her face really close to mine and rubbed my nose with hers before saying, "I know it's your Mother who should have been here instead of me. But, this is what you have now, I am what you have... I may not be Anna, but, I am her sister and I love you. I loved you the moment I heard your voice on the phone."

"I think I'll never find her. This is the last leg of my search. If she wanted to see me, she knows where she left me," I replied.

"Just remember that you have a place to come home to when you need the warmth and love of a family – your real family," Sarah said.

Family. I realized that the word had found a new meaning in my heart, it sounded... Precious. I repeated the word over and over in my mind, exactly the way Aunt Sarah said it in her honey-rich voice and I swear, I could soar above the clouds that had slowly made descent to wrap the city in a rich velvet blanket.

***

Epilogue

I now understand that when life deals you bad cards so early in life, you can only play that hand as best as you can. With grace, I find that life is best lived in the moment, and so I no longer pine for a fairy-tale ending.

Not a single one of my abusers was brought to justice. I was too young, too afraid and too confused to know what to do. Fifteen or so years after telling my father about what happened, I found out that he had told his wife and confronted his son about it. I never received an apology nor did anyone in the family talk to me about it.

While I still sometimes wonder about the three children that I have mothered for eight years, I still prefer to stay as far away as possible to avoid the risk of running into my abusive ex-boyfriend.

Someday, in another time, another place and perhaps another dimension, justice will be served. I hold on to that hope because I know that my God never sleeps.

Sadly, I live in a place where poverty and corruption abound, mental health issues are not being given a priority and there are no solid post-traumatic therapy programs or systems in place for child sexual abuse survivors. But even sadder is the fact that abuse survivors suffer the effects all throughout their lives. I have been living with tremendous guilt, anger, bitterness, self-pity, self-doubt and have a habit if expressing my "sense of failure" through fits of blind rage and depression. It is also challenging to maintain a loving, peaceful and meaningful relationship because I have huge trust issues and insecurities. For a long time, I could not survive a day without alcohol numbing my system.

I never really understood myself and have come to believe that I was just born rebellious, stubborn and *that* depraved, until I started reading articles about child sexual abuse. It had been difficult to acknowledge that the darker side of me might have been a result of what I have gone through, but when I finally came to terms with it, I finally learned how to start making peace with myself.

In the meantime, by the grace of God, I will my heart to forgive – forgive my abusers, forgive my biological mother, forgive my father and most of all, forgive myself. The anguish and bitterness of those years have left scars too deep that each one seared through my very soul, but those ordeals contributed in moulding the person that I am today. Letting go may not be easy because there are still days that the memories would come crashing back and I would be tempted to go on a blind rampage – driving inebriated, smashing items on walls and on the floor, physically inflicting pain on myself and thinking about committing suicide- but I take little steps forward everyday and I understand that it is a process. Healing won't happen overnight. In fact, I also acknowledge that complete healing may not even happen at all... But I am grateful for each day that allows me to move forward. I am thankful for having a partner who understands what I have been through and who helps me realize that I am beautiful inside and out, worthy of love, respect and dignity. I am blessed to have found someone who loves me for who I am and accepts my brokenness as part of the woman whose heart he had captivated. I often ask him what took him so long to arrive, but thinking about it, he couldn't have arrived at a more perfect time in my life. I love him with all my heart and soul.

Aunt Sarah, to be honest I don't know exactly where she lives. There are days she would be on the northern part of the country, other times she would be down south. Once in a while, she stays with me for a few days and it is on those days that I discover the things I would not have had we never met. She would tell me bits and pieces about the people who are a part of who I am – my grandfather, Anna, herself. I find it heartwarming to know how much alike we are in so many ways, such as how we both don't stay in one place for long. "It's in our genes, my love. We're nomads," she would tell me and I would understand exactly what she means. It also feels great to know that there is someone who understands why I am what I am.

I may have turned the final page and reached the final leg of my search for Anna, but my heart will always long to see her. Anna's memories will haunt me forever. She will always be etched in my being, like thread sewn through the fibers of my very soul. I see her in me when I stare at my reflection in the mirror. I see her on the color of my skin, I see her on the perk of my butt, I see her on the curve and fullness of my lips, I see her beneath the almond shape of my eyes – I see her in my soul. I know that somewhere, in some unchartered crevice of this world, she lives day after day wondering about me, too. Perhaps it is just a matter of time before she would find the courage and bravery to find me. Or perhaps not. Who can tell what tomorrow would bring?

As of today, there are roughly seven billion people sharing earth's space, air and water. Each one of them is on a journey through life, chasing dreams and holding on to promises, rebuilding broken lives and running away from the dark, paving and inching their way towards a better tomorrow.

I am releasing my own demons of times gone by and seizing the opportunity to find my own corner, my own fortress, my own calm and peace. Life is *not* unfair. We just have to learn to let go of the things that weigh us down and move on from situations that we cannot control.

Life is good. In the end, you only have yourself to search for and find...

***

                                  -THE END-

Message from the Author

I understand that there are many child sexual abuse survivors who may still be afraid to come out, speak and publicly advocate against child sexual abuse. While it may be the best thing to do to prevent any more children from falling into the hands of predators, it still takes so much courage, strength and bravery to do so. Being unexpectedly in the public eye can be overwhelming and carrying out such task can be daunting. If you ever told anyone and you are being convinced to speak out, remember that you are no longer a victim and that you ALWAYS have a choice on the matter. Never feel "trapped" again. You are the only one who has the right to decide for yourself.

Writing this book connected me to organizations, individuals and agencies that have shown great interest in my story. They have been convincing me to speak out and for a short period of time, I easily slipped into the "victim state of mind", as I call it. I felt caged once more - trapped, confused and caught on the edge of a precipice. It took just one email from another Author for me to realize that I am now an adult and have every right to choose what I feel is right for me. I choose to silently advocate and this book should be enough for now. If one, two or three child sexual abuse survivors get a chance to read Finding Anna and decide to come out, seek help or reach out to other victims and survivors, then I have made a contribution, albeit in a small way. This is my choice and this is what I think is right for me at the moment.

Whether you are a victim who would like to seek help and intervention, a survivor looking for a support group or an individual who is interested in supporting anti-child abuse advocacies, there are a number of organizations you can call or get in touch with. If you want the list, I can most certainly provide it for you. Just get in touch with me through email.

My prayer is that you would take that step towards finding help, healing and peace. People like us have suffered immensely, but there is hope for all of us. There certainly is.

Please visit my website at http://findinganna.com for more resources and information on child, sexual and domestic abuse. Alternatively, you can follow me on Facebook.Com/tklleone. I'm also on Twitter and Google+.

All the best,

Trish Kaye Lleone

***

Trish Kaye Lleone is a new Author from the Philippines who writes stories that she hopes would inspire, empower and encourage women to continue to hope and love in the midst of battling socio-economic, psychological, physical and emotional crises.

To connect with Trish, follow her on her social media networks

Printed in Great Britain
by Amazon